By Dr. Javnyuy Joybert

THE BUSINESS IDEA HANDBOOK

Dr. Javnyuy Joybert

THE BUSINESS IDEA HANDBOOK:

Finding Business Ideas in Unexpected Places

How to Uncover Hidden Business Ideas and Opportunities

Dr. Javnyuy Joybert

By Dr. Javnyuy Joybert

By Dr. Javnyuy Joybert

TABLE OF CONTENTS

INTRODUCTION

Welcome to *"The Business Idea Handbook: Finding Business Ideas in Unexpected Places* by Dr. Javnyuy Joybert"!

In this book, we will explore a variety of techniques and strategies for finding business ideas in unexpected places, and turning those ideas into successful businesses.

Whether you are a seasoned entrepreneur looking for your next big venture, or a beginner looking to start your first business, this book will provide you with the tools and guidance you need to identify and pursue new

Your branded COMPETENCE help people to notice you & to know when to need you.

What are you branding?

By Dr. Javnyuy Joybert

opportunities.

We will explore how to think creatively and out of the box, and how to turn your passions and interests into profitable businesses.

We will also provide practical advice on how to research and evaluate potential business ideas, and how to develop a solid business plan to bring your ideas to life.

Whether you are looking to start a small side hustle or a large-scale enterprise, *"The Business Idea Handbook"* will help you find the inspiration and guidance you need to turn your business dreams into reality.

PART ONE

UNEXPECTED PLACES TO UNCOVER HIDDEN BUSINESS IDEAS

1. What knowledge or skills did you acquire during your education (or through life) that you could use to start a business and generate income?

To explain further, I would like to clarify that "monetizing" refers to the process of *turning a product or service into a source of revenue.*

In the context of your education, this could mean using the knowledge or skills you acquired in school to start a business that provides a product or service in exchange for payment.

For example, if you studied marketing in school, you could use your knowledge and skills to start a marketing consulting business, helping small businesses with their marketing strategy in exchange for a fee. Or if you studied engineering, you could use your expertise to start a business that designs and manufactures products for a specific industry.

In general, the key is to identify the knowledge or skills that you have acquired during your education and see how you can use them to create value for others in a way that allows you to generate income.

This may involve setting up a traditional business, or it could involve finding ways to monetize your skills through freelancing or consulting.

Public Relations:

Knowing how to manage the reputation of a business or organization through effective communication with the media and the public can be valuable for a business agency.

Event Planning:

Being able to plan and execute events, such as conferences, trade shows, and fundraising programs, can be a useful skill for a business agency.

Advertising:

Understanding how to create and place ads in various media, such as print, radio, and television, can be useful for a business agency that helps clients with their advertising campaigns. These same skills can also be used in the online marketplace to generate income via selling your skills in Facebook Ads, Instagram Ads or Google Ads. Many businesses today are in dire need for advertising experts.

Social Media Management:

Knowing how to create and manage social media accounts, create content, and engage with followers can be valuable for a business agency that helps clients with their social media presence.

Content Creation:

Being able to create written, visual, or audio content for websites, social media, or other platforms can be useful for a business agency that helps clients with their content marketing efforts.

By Dr. Javnyuy Joybert

Public Speaking:

Being able to deliver presentations and speak publicly can be valuable for a business agency that represents clients at events or conferences.

Translation:

Being multilingual and able to accurately translate written content can be useful for a business agency that works with clients in multiple languages. Note here that interpretation also falls in this category, but interpretation deals with what is spoken; while translation deals with what is written. In both cases, your multilingual skills can be monetised.

Interpersonal Skills:

Having strong interpersonal skills, such as the ability to listen, empathize, and negotiate, can be valuable for a business agency that works with clients and partners. According to global organizations, the top 7 power skills that will be relevant in the post Covid-19 era are: emotional intelligence, communication, adaptability, collaboration, creativity, leadership and time management.

Research:

Being able to conduct research, analyse data, and draw conclusions can be useful for a business agency that helps clients with market research or other types of data analysis.

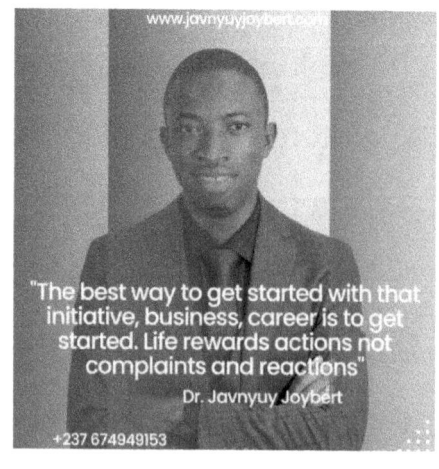

www.javnyuyjoybert.com

"The best way to get started with that initiative, business, career is to get started. Life rewards actions not complaints and reactions"

Dr. Javnyuy Joybert

+237 674949153

By Dr. Javnyuy Joybert

Project Management:

Knowing how to plan, organize, and execute projects efficiently can be valuable for a business agency that helps clients with various types of projects.

Writing:

Being able to write clearly and effectively can be valuable for a business that needs to create written content for its website, social media, or marketing materials.

Editing:

Being able to edit written or visual content for clarity, accuracy, and style can be useful for a business that produces a lot of written or visual content.

Interior Design:

Knowing how to design and arrange interior

spaces can be valuable for a business that offers interior design services.

Landscaping:

Being able to design and maintain outdoor spaces can be useful for a business that offers landscaping services.

Personal Training:

Knowing how to design and implement exercise programs and provide guidance on nutrition and other health-related topics can be valuable for a business that offers personal training services.

Teaching:

Being able to plan and deliver effective lessons and provide guidance and support to students can be valuable for a business that offers tutoring or other educational services.

Cooking:

Knowing how to prepare and cook a variety of dishes is a valuable asset for a business that offers catering or food-related services.

2. What is missing in your community that you can provide as a service/product?

What services or products could you offer to meet a need or fill a gap in your community?

Identifying a need or gap in your community and offering a service or product to meet that need is a common yet significant way to start a business.

Here is a practical process for how this can work:

Identify The Need Or Gap:

The first step is to identify a need or gap in your community that you could potentially fill with a product or service. This could be a need for a particular type of product that is not currently available, or a lack of a certain service.

Research The Market:

Once you have identified a potential opportunity, it is important to do some research to determine if there is actually a demand for your product or service. This could involve talking to potential customers, surveying the market, and analyzing competitors. This state is vital because products and services need a market. If there's no demand, then there's no need to open certain businesses. So make sure what you want to sell is *needed.*

Develop A Business Plan:

Based on your research, you should develop a detailed business plan that outlines how you will create and deliver your product or service, as well as how you will generate revenue and profits.

Launch Your Business:

Once you have a solid business plan in place, you can begin to put your plan into action. This may involve sourcing materials, building a team, and marketing your product or service to potential customers.

Monitor And Adjust:

As you start your business, it is important to monitor your progress and adjust your strategy as needed. This may involve revising your business plan, adapting to changes in the market, making changes improve chances

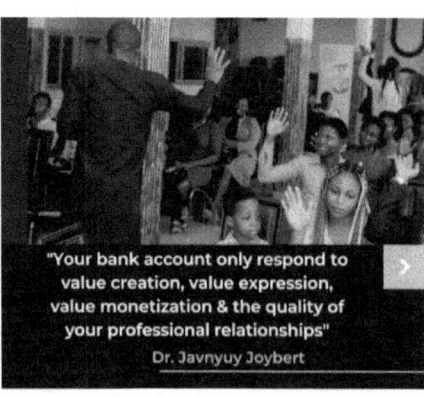

"Your bank account only respond to value creation, value expression, value monetization & the quality of your professional relationships"
Dr. Javnyuy Joybert

or other to your of

success.

Summarily, you need a product or service, you need a market which will buy this product or service, you need a written plan, you need to launch your business, and then monitor and evaluate its progress.

3. What products or services could you create and offer using your vocational skills or manual dexterity

Vocational skills, or skills that are specific to a particular trade or profession, can often be used to create products or offer services that can be sold to generate income. If you have developed specific skills or manual dexterity through your education or training, you may be able to use these skills to start a business or offer a service to others.

For example, if you are skilled in woodworking or carpentry, you could make and sell handmade furniture, crafts, or other wood products. If you are skilled in sewing, you could make and sell handmade clothings or accessories. Or if you are skilled in a particular trade, such as plumbing or electrical work, you could offer your services to homeowners or businesses in need of repairs or maintenance.

In general, the key is to identify the skills you have developed with your hands and think about how you can use these skills to create value for others. This could involve making physical products, offering a service, or a combination of both

Starting a business using a vocational skill can be a rewarding and fulfilling way to generate income and achieve financial independence.

Here are some practical steps for how you can get started:

Identify Your Skill:

The first step is to identify the specific vocational skill that you want to use to start a business. This could be a skill that you have developed through your education or training, or it could be a hobby or passion that you have turned into a skill through practice and experience.

Research The Market:

Once you have identified your skill, it is important to do some research to determine if there is a demand for the product or service you want to offer. This could involve talking to potential customers, surveying the market, and analyzing competitors.

Develop A Business Plan:

Based on your research, you should develop a detailed business plan that outlines how you will create and deliver your product or service, as well as how you will generate revenue and profits.

Launch Your Business:

Once you have a solid business plan in place, you can begin to put your plan into action. This may involve sourcing materials, building a team, and marketing your product or service to potential customers.

Monitor And Adjust:

As you start your business, it is important to monitor your progress and adjust your strategy as needed. This may involve revising your business plan, adapting to changes in the market, or making other changes to improve your chances of success. Someone has said that the illiterate of the 21st century is not the person who doesn't know how to read and write; but he who cannot unlearn, learn and relearn. Business demands a high spirit of adaptability. Learn to adopt new strategies as you evaluate your progress.

By Dr. Javnyuy Joybert

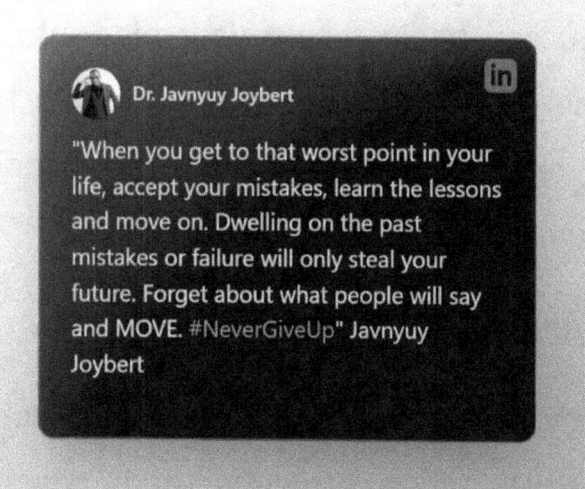

Dr. Javnyuy Joybert

"When you get to that worst point in your life, accept your mistakes, learn the lessons and move on. Dwelling on the past mistakes or failure will only steal your future. Forget about what people will say and MOVE. #NeverGiveUp" Javnyuy Joybert

4. What products or services do people frequently request from you that you could start offering in exchange for payment?

Identifying products or services that people frequently request from you is a good starting point for starting a business. If people are already asking for something from you, it is likely that there is a demand for it, and you may be able to generate income by offering it as a paid service or product.

Here are some steps for how you can turn something that people frequently ask from you into a business:

Identify The Product Or Service:

The first step is to identify the product or service that people are frequently asking from you. This could be something as simple as a particular type of advice or guidance, or it could be a more complex product or service that you have developed through your skills and expertise.

Research The Market:

Once you have identified the product or service that people are frequently asking from you, it is important to do some research to determine if there is a demand for it in the market. This could involve talking to potential customers, surveying the market, and analyzing competitors.

Develop A Business Plan:

Based on your research, you should develop a detailed business plan that outlines how you will create and deliver your product or service, as well as how you will generate revenue and profits.

Launch Your Business:

Once you have a solid business plan in place, you can begin to put your plan into action. This may involve sourcing materials, building a team, and marketing your product or service to potential customers.

Monitor And Adjust:

As you start your business, it is important to monitor your progress and adjust your strategy as needed. This may involve revising your business plan, adapting to changes in the market, or making other changes to improve your chances of success.

5. What digital skills do you possess that you could use to start an online agency and generate income?

Starting an online agency can be a lucrative way to monetize your digital skills and generate income. An online agency is a business that provides a product or service to clients over the internet.

There are many different types of online agencies, each offering a unique product or service based on the skills and expertise of the business owner.

Here are ten examples of digital skills that could be used to start an online agency:

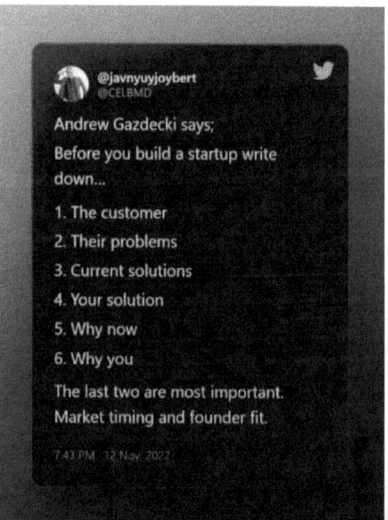

Web Design:

If you have skills in web design, you could start an online agency that designs and builds websites for clients.

Graphic Design:

If you have skills in graphic design, you could start an online agency that creates logos, branding materials, and other visual assets for clients.

Social media management:

If you have skills in social media management, you could start an online agency that helps businesses manage their social media presence and engage with their audience.

Content Marketing:

If you have skills in content marketing, you

could start an online agency that helps businesses create and distribute valuable, relevant, and consistent content to attract and retain a clearly defined audience.

SEO:

If you have skills in Search Engine Optimization (SEO), you can start an online agency that helps businesses improve their ranking in search engine results and drive traffic to their websites.

Email Marketing:

If you have skills in email marketing, you could start an online agency that helps businesses create and send effective email campaigns to their customers and prospects.

Online Advertising:

If you have skills in online advertising, you could start an online agency that helps businesses advertise their products or services on platforms such as Google Ads or Facebook Ads.

E-Commerce:

If you have skills in e-commerce, you could start an online agency that helps businesses set up and manage their online stores.

Video Production:

If you have skills in video production, you can start an online agency that creates video content for businesses.

Online Tutoring:

If you have expertise in a particular subject or skill, you could start an online agency that offers tutoring or teaching services to clients

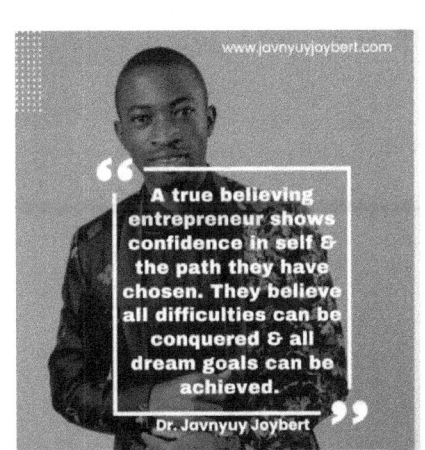

www.javnyuyjoybert.com

" A true believing entrepreneur shows confidence in self & the path they have chosen. They believe all difficulties can be conquered & all dream goals can be achieved. "

Dr. Javnyuy Joybert

By Dr. Javnyuy Joybert

over the internet.

In general, the key is to identify your unique digital skills and think about how you can use them to create value for others in a way that allows you to generate income. With the right combination of skills and effort, you can turn your digital expertise into a successful online agency.

6. What ideas keep running through your mind that you can research more about them and turn into a business?

What business ideas have you been thinking about that you could further research and potentially turn into a reality?

Having business ideas is the first step to starting a business, but it is important to carefully research and evaluate these ideas before moving forward. Here are some steps for how you can turn your business ideas into a reality.

There are several ways to make good use of business ideas that run through your mind:

Research And Evaluate:

The first step is to research and evaluate your business ideas to determine if they are viable and worth pursuing. This could involve talking to potential customers, surveying the market, and analyzing competitors. This is inevitable because your business idea must be relevant to the present dispensation. Many times, I like telling people this: "*The ideas that brought you from 2013 to 2023 cannot take you from 2023 to 2033.*"

Develop A Business Plan:

If you determine that a business idea is worth pursuing, the next step is to develop a detailed business plan that outlines how you will create and deliver your product or service, as well as how you will generate revenue and profits.

Seek Feedback And Advice:

It can be helpful to seek feedback and advice from others as you evaluate your business ideas. This could include seeking the advice of a mentor, consulting with a business coach or advisor, or soliciting feedback from potential customers or industry experts.

Test Your Ideas:

Before launching a full-scale business, it can be helpful to test your ideas in a smaller scale to see if they are viable. This could involve creating a prototype or offering a limited number of products or services to a small group of customers.

Take action:

Once you have thoroughly researched and evaluated your business ideas, it is important to take action and start bringing your ideas to life. This may involve sourcing materials, building a team, and marketing your product or service to potential customers.

Monitor and adjust:

As you start your business, it is important to monitor your progress and adjust your strategy as needed. This may involve revising your business plan, adapting to changes in the market, or making other changes to improve your chances of success.

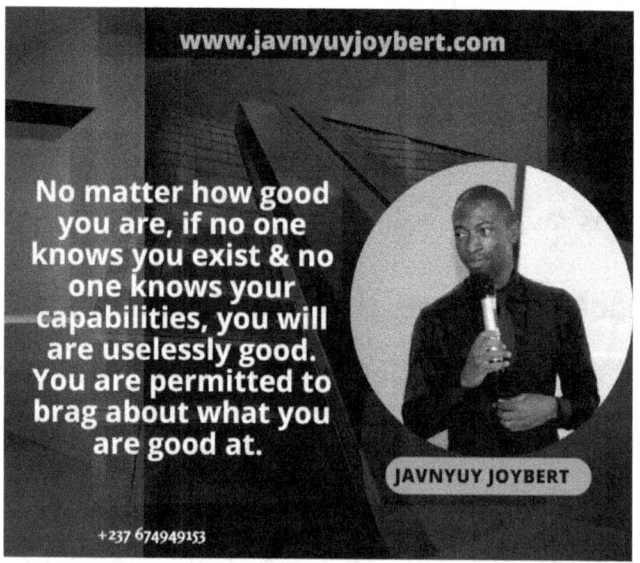

www.javnyuyjoybert.com

No matter how good you are, if no one knows you exist & no one knows your capabilities, you will are uselessly good. You are permitted to brag about what you are good at.

JAVNYUY JOYBERT

+237 674949153

By Dr. Javnyuy Joybert

7. What products or services are being poorly provided by others in your area that you could do better and serve better, turn into a successful business?

Identifying products or services that are being poorly provided by others in your area is a common way to identify a business opportunity. If you can offer a better version of a product or service that is currently being poorly provided, you may be able to attract customers and generate income.

Here are some steps for how you can turn a poorly provided product or service into a successful business:

Identify The Opportunity:

The first step is to identify a product or service that is being poorly provided by others in your area. This could be a product that is of poor quality, or a service that is not meeting the needs or expectations of customers. Or a product about which many consumers are complaining.

Research The Market:

Once you have identified the opportunity, it is important to do some research to determine if there is a demand for a better version of the product or service. This could involve talking to potential customers, surveying the market, and analyzing competitors.

Develop A Unique Value Proposition:

To differentiate your business from others, you should develop a Unique Value Proposition (UVP) that clearly communicates the benefits of your product or service. This could include highlighting the superior quality, convenience, or value that your product or service offers as compared to others.

Create A Business Plan:

Based on your research, you should develop a detailed business plan that outlines how you will create and deliver your product or service, as well as how you will generate revenue and profits. You must be clear about what you will bring in that doesn't already exist.

Launch Your Business:

Once you have a solid business plan in place, you can begin to put your plan into action. This may involve sourcing materials, building a team, and marketing your product or service to potential customers.

Monitor And Adjust:

As you start your business, it is important to monitor your progress and adjust your strategy as needed. This may involve revising your business plan, adapting to changes in the market, or making other changes to improve your chances of success.

Starting a business by offering a better version of a product or service that is currently being poorly provided is a common way to enter the market and generate income. By identifying a gap in the market and filling it with a superior product or service, you can differentiate your business from others and attract customers. Steve Jobs and Apple entered the marketplace through this strategy. The rest is history as to where Apple is today.

8. What are people generally glamouring about around you that you can package and sell?

What products or services are people frequently expressing interest in or admiring around you that you could package and sell?

Identifying products or services that people are frequently expressing interest in or admiring around you is a good starting point for starting a business. If people are already showing interest in something, it is likely that there is a demand for it, and you may be able to generate income by offering it for sale.

Here are some steps for how you can turn something that people are generally glamouring about into a business:

Identify The Product Or Service:

The first step is to identify the product or service that people are frequently expressing interest in or admiring. This could be something as simple as a particular type of product or service, or it could be a more complex product or service that you have developed through your skills and expertise.

By Dr. Javnyuy Joybert

Research The Market:

Once you have identified the product or service that people are expressing interest in, it is important to do some research to determine if there is a demand for it in the market. This could involve talking to potential customers, surveying the market, and analyzing competitors.

Develop A Business Plan:

Based on your research, you should develop a detailed business plan that outlines how you will create and deliver your product or service, as well as how you will generate revenue and profits.

Launch Your Business:

Once you have a solid business plan in place, you can begin to put your plan into action. This may involve sourcing materials, building a team, and marketing your

Starting a business by offering a product or service that people are frequently expressing interest in or admiring is a common way to enter the market and generate income. By identifying a gap in the market and filling it with a product or service that meets the needs or interests of your target audience, you can differentiate your business from others and attract customers.

To do this effectively, it is important to conduct thorough research and analysis to ensure that there is a demand for your product or service and that you are able to differentiate yourself from competitors. This may involve talking to potential customers, surveying the market, and analyzing competitors to understand their strengths and weaknesses.

Once you have a clear understanding of the market, you should develop a unique value proposition that clearly communicates the benefits of your product or service. This could include highlighting the superior quality, convenience, or value that your product or service offers compared to others.

With a solid business plan in place, you can then begin to put your plan into action by sourcing materials, building a team, and marketing your product or service to potential customers. As you start your business, it is important to monitor your progress and adjust your strategy as needed to ensure that you are meeting the needs of your customers and achieving your business goals.

By Dr. Javnyuy Joybert

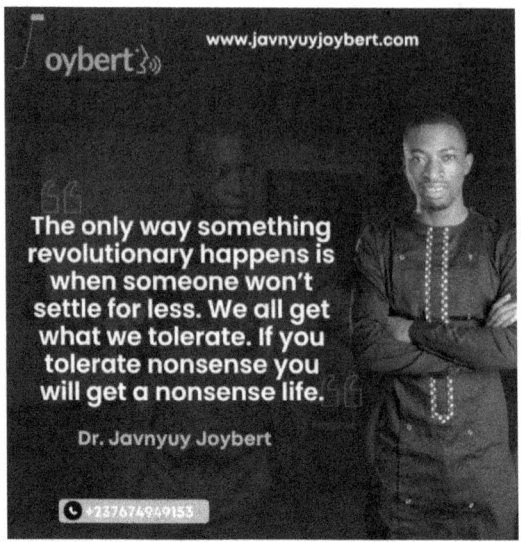

9. What are your interests and passions that you could turn into a business?

Starting a business based on your interests and passions is a great way to enter the market and generate income. By offering a product or service that aligns with your interests and passions, you are likely to be more motivated and engaged in your work, which can increase your chances of success.

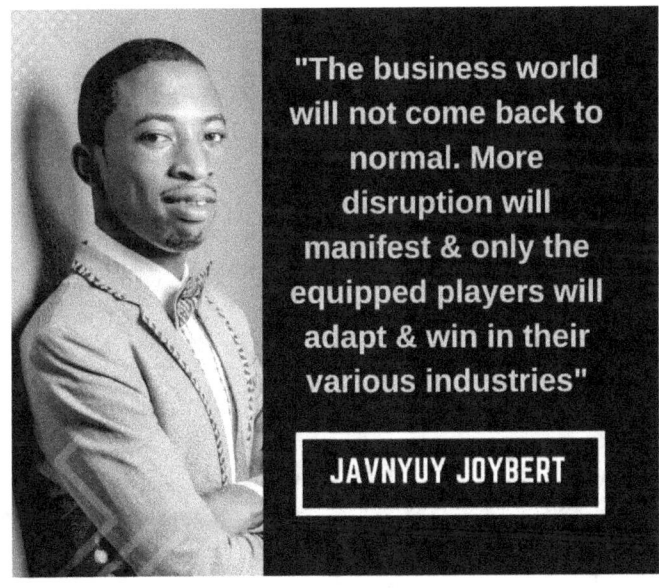

"The business world will not come back to normal. More disruption will manifest & only the equipped players will adapt & win in their various industries"

JAVNYUY JOYBERT

By Dr. Javnyuy Joybert

Here are some steps for how you can turn your interests and passions into a business:

Identify Your Interests And Passions:

The first step is to identify your interests and passions and think about how you could turn them into a business. This could be a product or service that you are already knowledgeable about or experienced in, or it could be something that you are eager to learn more about and explore.

Research The Market:

Once you have identified your interests and passions, it is important to do some research to determine if there is a demand for them in the market. This could involve talking to potential customers, surveying the market, and analyzing competitors.

Develop A Business Plan:

Based on your research, you should develop a detailed business plan that outlines how you will create and deliver your product or service, as well as how you will generate revenue and profits.

Launch Your Business:

Once you have a solid business plan in place, you can begin to put your plan into action. This may involve sourcing materials, building a team, and marketing your product or service to potential customers.

Monitor And Adjust:

As you start your business, it is important to monitor your progress and adjust your strategy as needed. This may involve revising your business plan, adapting to changes in the market, or making other changes to improve your chances of success.

Starting a business based on your interests and passions can be a rewarding and fulfilling way to enter the market and generate income. By offering a product or service that aligns with your interests and passions, you are likely to be more motivated and engaged in your work, which can increase your chances of success.

To turn your interests and passions into a business, it is important to conduct thorough research and analysis to ensure that there is a demand for your product or service and that you are able to differentiate yourself from competitors. This may involve talking to potential customers, surveying the market, and analyzing competitors to understand their strengths and weaknesses.

Once you have a clear understanding of the market, you should develop a unique value proposition that clearly communicates the benefits of your product or service. This could include highlighting the superior quality, convenience, or value that your product or service offers compared to others.

With a solid business plan in place, you can then begin to put your plan into action by sourcing materials, building a team, and marketing your product or service to potential customers. As you start your business, it is important to monitor your progress and adjust your strategy as needed to ensure that you

Make it happen now, not tomorrow. I will do it "tomorrow" is a loser's excuse. The genius of doing it now is magical.

Dr. Javnyuy Joybert +237674949153 www.javnyuyjoybert.com

are meeting the needs of your customers and achieving your business goals.

It is also important to remember that starting a business requires hard work, dedication, and persistence. While it can be rewarding, it can also be challenging at times, so it is important to be prepared for the ups and downs that come with entrepreneurship. However, with the right combination of skills, passion, and effort, you can turn your interests and passions into a successful business.

In this first part of this book, we have show you in practical ways how to find business ideas in the unlikely places and transform thm into reality. Let's see what Part Two offers.

PART TWO

15 EXAMPLES OF INTERESTS AND PASSIONS PEOPLE CAN START BUSINESSES FROM

Art:

If you have a passion for art, you could start a business selling your own artwork, teaching art classes, or offering custom art commissions.

Cooking:

If you have a passion for cooking, you could start a catering business, a food truck, or a restaurant.

Photography:

If you have a passion for photography, you could start a photography business offering portrait sessions, event coverage, or commercial photography services.

Music:

If you have a passion for music, you could start a business offering music lessons, hosting concerts or music events, or selling musical instruments or equipment.

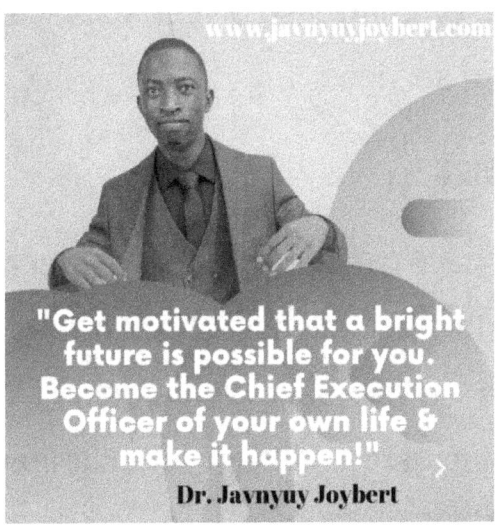

"Get motivated that a bright future is possible for you. Become the Chief Execution Officer of your own life & make it happen!"
Dr. Javnyuy Joybert

Writing:

If you have a passion for writing, you could start a business offering writing services, such as ghostwriting, editing, or content creation.

Fashion:

If you have a passion for fashion, you could start a business selling your own clothing designs, offering fashion consulting services, or styling services.

Gardening:

If you have a passion for gardening, you could start a business offering landscaping services, selling plants or gardening supplies, or offering garden design consultations.

Fitness:

If you have a passion for fitness, you could start a business offering personal training services, hosting fitness classes, or selling

DR. JAVNYUY JOYBERT

"You can be born with natural talents but it doesn't mean you are skillful. For example because you are fluent does not mean you are a public speaker or a trainer. You have to develop your talents into valuable skills"

fitness equipment or supplements.

Beauty:

If you have a passion for beauty, you could start a business offering makeup, hair, or nail services, or selling beauty products.

Home Improvement:

If you have a passion for home improvement, you could start a business offering handyman services, home renovations, or selling home improvement products.

Pet Care:

If you have a passion for pet care, you could start a business offering pet sitting, dog walking, or grooming services.

Travel:

If you have a passion for travel, you could start a business offering travel planning

By Dr. Javnyuy Joybert

services, hosting group trips, or selling travel products.

Crafting:

If you have a passion for crafting, you could start a business selling handmade products, hosting craft workshops, or offering custom craft projects.

Technology:

If you have a passion for technology, you could start a business offering tech support services, selling tech products, or offering tech consulting services.

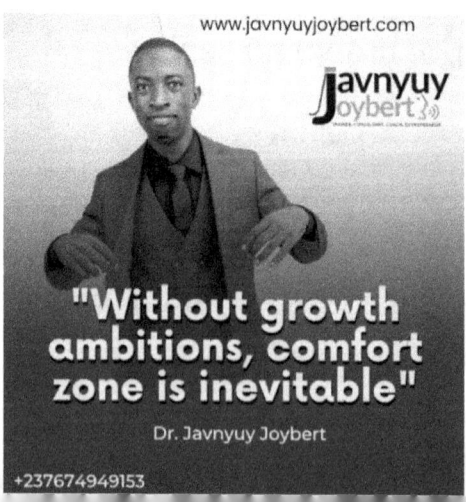

Education:

If you have a passion for education, you could start a business offering tutoring services, hosting educational workshops, or developing educational resources.

CONCLUSION

I believe that with the right combination of creativity, curiosity, and massive persistence, you can uncover hidden business ideas and opportunities that may not be immediately obvious.

By keeping an open mind and looking for opportunities in unexpected places, you can find new and innovative ways to solve problems and meet the needs of your customers.

I encourage you to continue learning and growing as an entrepreneur, and to never stop seeking out new and exciting business opportunities.

I hope that this second part of *The Business Idea Handbook* has provided you with the tools and guidance you need to turn your

By Dr. Javnyuy Joybert

business dreams into a reality.

Successful business owners and entrepreneurs are willing to take action and face their fears in order to start and grow

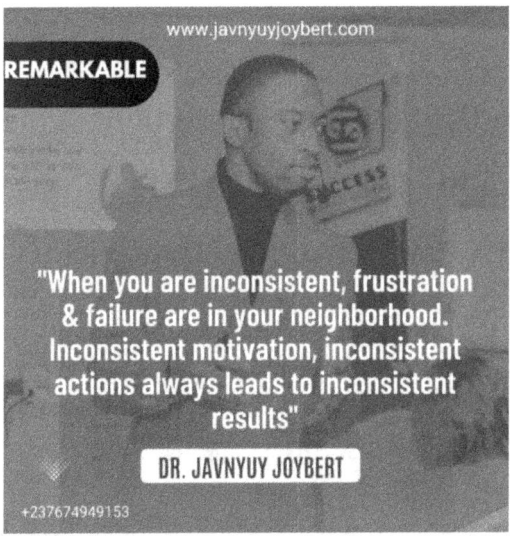

their businesses.

Without taking massive action, no business idea will be able to get off the ground and succeed. Those who are able to overcome their fears and take bold steps towards building their businesses are more likely to achieve success. In order to start and grow a successful business, it is important to be willing to take calculated risks, try new things, and be proactive in pursuing your goals.

Starting and running a successful business requires a willingness to take action and face challenges head-on. This often involves stepping outside of your comfort zone, taking risks, and trying new things. Successful business owners and entrepreneurs are not afraid to take massive action in pursuit of their goals, even if this means facing their fears and overcoming obstacles.

Without action, no business idea will be able to get off the ground and grow. It is important to be proactive in pursuing your business goals, and to take the necessary steps to bring your ideas to life. This may involve sourcing materials, building a team, marketing your product or service, and continually adapting to the changing needs of your customers and the market.

In order to succeed in business, it is also important to be resilient and persistent. There will inevitably be setbacks and challenges along the way, but those who are able to stay focused and continue moving forward are more likely to achieve success. By being willing to take action and face your fears, you can build a successful business that is able to thrive in the face of adversity.

APPENDIX 1: WRITING A BUSINESS PLAN

Here is a sample business plan for someone who is planning to start a social media management agency startup.

Use it as a sample to write a good business plan for any idea you want to start.

Executive Summary:

XYZ Social Media Management is a startup agency that will provide social media management services to small businesses and entrepreneurs. Our team of experts will help our clients create and implement social media strategies that will increase their online presence, engage their audience, and drive sales. We will offer a range of services, including social media account setup and optimization, content creation and curation, social media advertising, analytics and reporting.

Market Analysis:

The market for social media management services is growing rapidly, as more and more businesses recognize the importance of having a strong online presence. According to a recent survey, 90% of small businesses in the US use social media for marketing, and 75% of them reported that it has helped them increase sales. In addition, research shows that social media advertising is becoming more popular, with spending expected to reach $35 billion in the US by 2023.

Target Market:

Our target market is small businesses and entrepreneurs who do not have the time, resources, or expertise to manage their own social media accounts. We will focus on businesses in the local area, as well as those in specific industries such as retail, service, and hospitality. We will also target startups and solopreneurs who are looking to establish a strong online presence from the start.

Marketing Strategy:

We will use a combination of online and offline marketing to reach our target market. Our online marketing efforts will include social media advertising, email marketing, and content marketing through our blog and social media channels. We will also attend local networking events

Dr. Javnyuy Joybert

www.javnyuyjoybert.com
+237674949153

"You are an unethical & "yeye" business person if the only way you can sell your product is by painting your competitor black & spreading lies. You will not last!"

and collaborate with other businesses to reach potential clients.

Services And Pricing:

We will offer three packages for our social media management services: Basic, Premium, and Elite. The Basic package will include social media account setup and optimization, as well as monthly content creation and curation. The Premium package will include everything in the Basic package, as well as social media advertising and monthly analytics and reporting. The Elite package will include everything in the Premium package, as well as additional content creation and strategic planning. Prices for our packages will range from $500 to $1,500 per month.

By Dr. Javnyuy Joybert

Management and Staffing:

XYZ Social Media Management will be owned and operated by [Name], who has experience in social media management and marketing. [Name] will be responsible for business development, client relations, and team management. [Name] will also hire and manage a team of social media experts to handle the day-to-day management of clients' social media accounts.

Financial Plan:

Our financial plan includes revenue projections for the first three years of operation. We expect to generate $30,000 in revenue in 3 years.

With this clear and concise business plan, any serious entrepreneur can start and scale their business into a thriving one. Remember

By Dr. Javnyuy Joybert

it takes dedication, commitment, hard work and persistence.

APPENDIX 2: SAMPLE RESEARCH QUESTIONS

Sample research questions an entrepreneur can ask to determine if there is a demand for them in the market:

What are the current trends in the industry?

Who are the main competitors in the market?

What are the unique selling points of my product or service?

What are the pain points or unmet needs of my target market?

What are the pricing and distribution channels in the market?

How is the target market currently solving the problem that my product or service addresses?

What is the projected growth of the market?

What are the customer demographics and purchasing habits of my target market?

What are the market conditions and economic factors that may impact my business?

What are the cultural and societal factors that may influence the demand for my product or service?

APPENDIX 3: CREATING A STARTUP BUDGET

Developing a budget for your start-up is essential for ensuring that you have the resources you need to get your business up and running. This budget should include all of the expenses you will incur as you start your business, such as purchasing equipment or materials, paying for marketing and advertising, and covering any other costs.

By creating a start-up budget, you will be able to determine whether the funds you have saved or the loan you are seeking will be sufficient to support the launch of your business.

A start-up budget is a financial plan that outlines the expenses you will incur as you start your business. This budget is important because it helps you understand the financial resources you will need to get your business off the ground. By creating a start-up budget, you can determine how much money you need to start your business and where that money will be spent. This can be especially helpful if you are seeking funding from a bank or other lender, as you can use your budget to demonstrate your financial needs and how you plan to use the funds.

A start-up budget should include all of the costs associated with launching your business, such as rent or lease payments, equipment, supplies, marketing and advertising, salaries and benefits, taxes, legal and

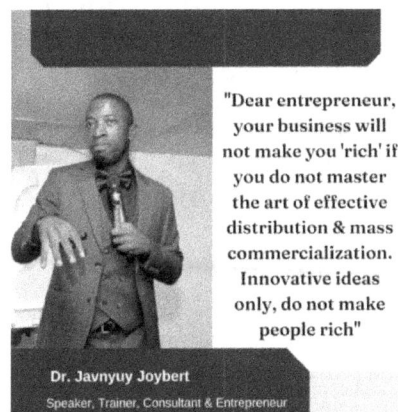

"Dear entrepreneur, your business will not make you 'rich' if you do not master the art of effective distribution & mass commercialization. Innovative ideas only, do not make people rich"

Dr. Javnyuy Joybert
Speaker, Trainer, Consultant & Entrepreneur

By Dr. Javnyuy Joybert

professional fees, travel and transportation, insurance, and any other miscellaneous expenses. By including all of these costs in your budget, you can get a comprehensive view of the financial resources you will need to start your business and make informed decisions about how to allocate those resources. Also, note that many of these costs may not be associated if you are starting really small and also starting from home. Make sure you are practical.

A start-up budget is also an important tool for managing your business's finances once you are up and running. By tracking your actual expenses against your budget, you can monitor your financial performance and make any necessary adjustments to ensure that you are staying on track financially. Overall, a start-up budget is a critical component of starting and running a successful business.

THE END

By Dr. Javnyuy Joybert